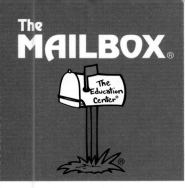

The MAILBOX®
The Education Center®

Literac ENVELOPE Centers

12 READY-TO-USE CENTERS

- **Matching Pictures**
- **Identifying What Doesn't Belong**
- **Matching Uppercase Letters**
- **Matching Lowercase Letters**
- **Identifying Rhyming Pictures**
- **Identifying Beginning Sounds**

Build Basic Literacy Skills!

Written by Ada Goren

Managing Editor: Allison E. Ward

Editorial Team: Becky S. Andrews, Kimberley Bruck, Karen P. Shelton, Diane Badden, Thad H. McLaurin, Sharon Murphy, Lynn Drolet, Karen A. Brudnak, Hope Rodgers, Dorothy C. McKinney

Production Team: Lori Henry, Pam Crane, Rebecca Saunders, Jennifer Tipton Cappoen, Chris Curry, Sarah Foreman, Theresa Lewis Goode, Clint Moore, Greg D. Rieves, Barry Slate, Donna K. Teal, Zane Williard, Tazmen Carlisle, Marsha Heim, Lynette Dickerson, Mark Rainey

www.themailbox.com

Another Fine Product From the Learning Centers Club®

Table of Contents

How to Use 3

Center Checklist 4

12 Envelope Centers

Skills

Visual discrimination: matching pictures.. 5

Visual discrimination: identifying what does not belong 15

Matching: uppercase letters 25

Matching: lowercase letters 37

Identifying rhyming pictures... 49

Identifying rhyming pictures... 59

Identifying rhyming pictures... 69

Identifying beginning sound /m/... 79

Identifying beginning sound /s/.. 89

Identifying beginning sound /f/... 99

Identifying beginning sound /l/... 109

Identifying beginning sound /n/...119

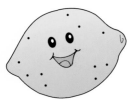

©2006 The Mailbox®
All rights reserved.
ISBN10 #1-56234-705-5 • ISBN13 #978-156234-705-5

Manufactured in the United States
10 9 8 7 6 5 4 3 2 1

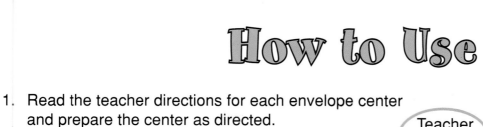

How to Use

1. Read the teacher directions for each envelope center and prepare the center as directed.

2. Use the center as directed on the teacher directions.

3. Provide more practice using the take-home parent page.

4. Use the reproducible checklist on page 4 to keep track of each student's progress.

Teacher Directions

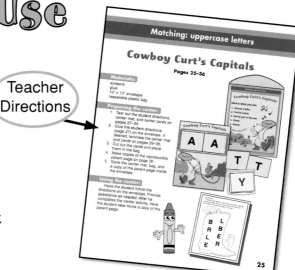

Envelope Center

Center Mat

Targeted Literacy Skill

Student Directions

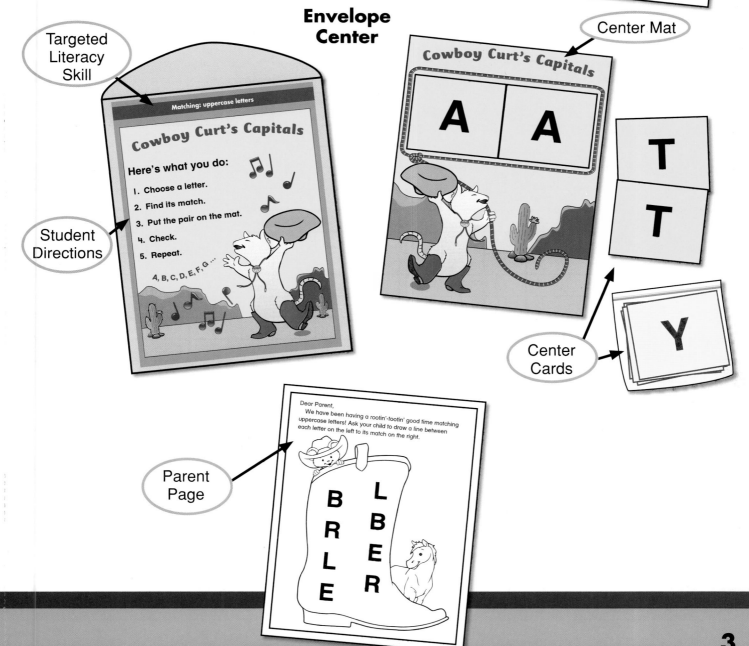

Center Cards

Parent Page

Envelope Center Checklist

Student	Fish-Tank Twins: Visual discrimination—matching pictures	Flowers in Bloom: Visual discrimination—identifying what does not belong	Cowboy Curt's Capitals: Matching—uppercase letters	Lowercase Lemonade: Matching—lowercase letters	Starring...Rhymes! Identifying rhyming pictures	Rub-a-Dub Tub: Identifying rhyming pictures	Royal Rhyming: Identifying rhyming pictures	Mouse's Masterpiece: Identifying beginning sound /m/	Silly Seal: Identifying beginning sound /s/	Fox's Football: Identifying beginning sound /f/	Lion's Lollipop: Identifying beginning sound /l/	What's in the Nest? Identifying beginning sound /n/

4

Fish-Tank Twins

Pages 5–14

Materials:

scissors
glue
10" x 13" envelope
resealable plastic bag

Preparing the center:

1. Tear out the student directions, center mat, and center cards on pages 7–14.
2. Glue the student directions (page 7) on the envelope. If desired, laminate the center mat and cards on pages 9–14.
3. Cut out the cards and place them in the bag.
4. Make copies of the reproducible parent page on page 6.
5. Store the center mat, bag, and copies of the parent page inside the envelope.

Using the center:

Have the student follow the directions on the envelope. Provide assistance as needed. After he completes the center activity, have the student take home a copy of the parent page.

Dear Parent,
We have been matching pictures. Ask your child to look at the fish in the tank below and find the matching pairs. Then, if desired, have your child color each pair of fish a different color.

Dear Parent,

We have been matching pictures. Ask your child to look at the fish in the tank below and find the matching pairs. Then, if desired, have your child color each pair of fish a different color.

Note to the teacher: Use with the directions on page 5.

Fish-Tank Twins

Here's what you do:

1. Choose a fish.

2. Find its match.

3. Put the pair in the tank.

4. Check.

5. Repeat.

Fish-Tank Twins

Fish-Tank Twins

Fish-Tank Twins
TEC61027

Fish-Tank Twins
TEC61027

Fish-Tank Twins
TEC61027

Fish-Tank Twins
TEC61027

Fish-Tank Twins
TEC61027

Fish-Tank Twins
TEC61027

Fish-Tank Twins

Fish-Tank Twins
TEC61027

Fish-Tank Twins
TEC61027

Fish-Tank Twins
TEC61027

Fish-Tank Twins
TEC61027

Fish-Tank Twins
TEC61027

Fish-Tank Twins
TEC61027

Flowers in Bloom

Pages 15–24

Materials:

scissors
glue
10" x 13" envelope
large resealable plastic bag

Preparing the center:

1. Tear out the student directions, center mat, and center cards on pages 17–24.
2. Glue the student directions (page 17) on the envelope. If desired, laminate the center mat and cards on pages 19–24.
3. Cut out the cards and place them in the bag.
4. Make copies of the reproducible parent page on page 16.
5. Store the center mat, bag, and copies of the parent page inside the envelope.

Using the center:

Have the student follow the directions on the envelope. Provide assistance as needed. After she completes the center activity, have the student take home a copy of the parent page.

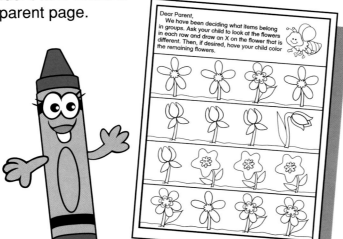

Dear Parent,
    We have been deciding what items belong in groups. Ask your child to look at the flowers in each row and draw an X on the flower that is different. Then, if desired, have your child color the remaining flowers.

Flowers in Bloom

Here's what you do:

1. Put a flower strip on the mat.

2. Put the bee on the flower that is different.

3. Check.

4. Repeat.

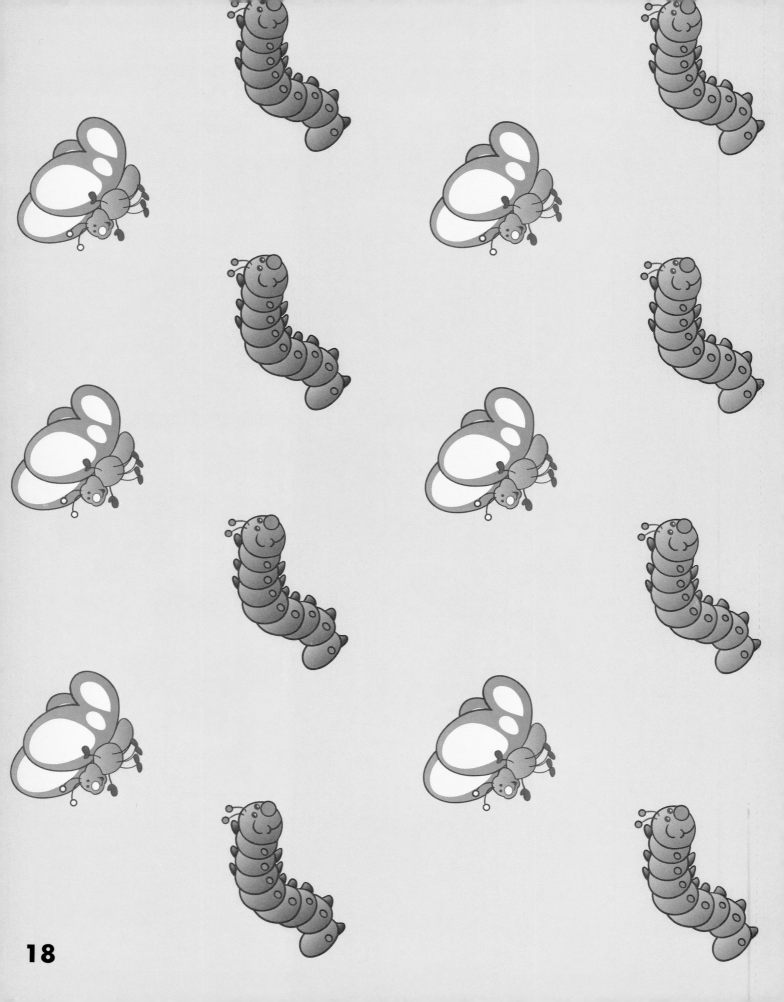

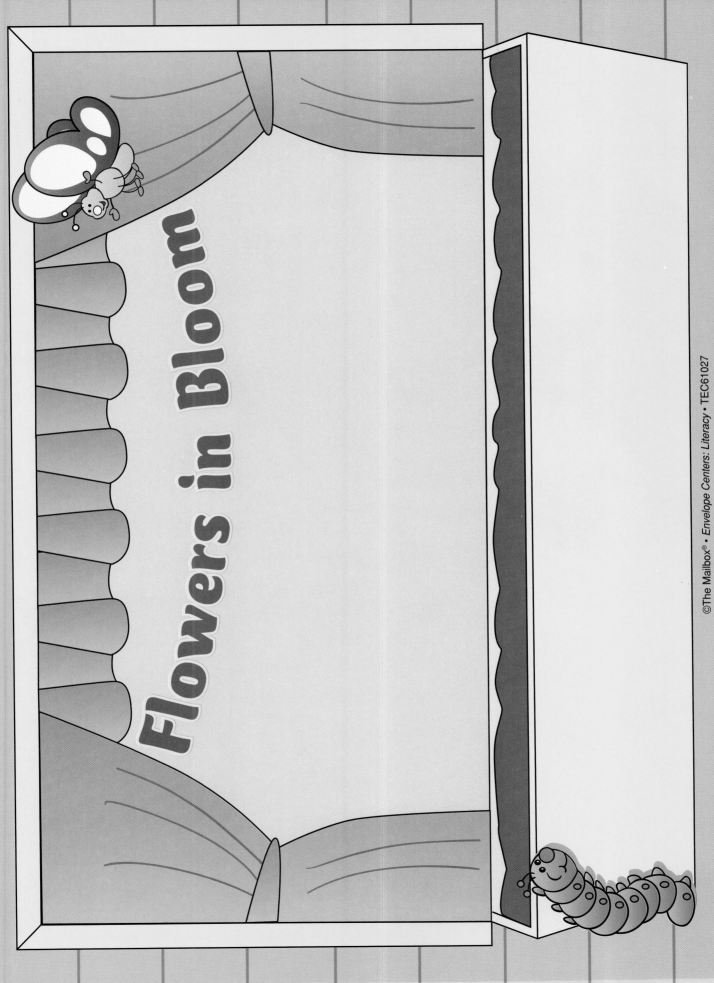

Flowers in Bloom

Flowers in Bloom

Flowers in Bloom
TEC61027

Flowers in Bloom
TEC61027

Flowers in Bloom
TEC61027

22

Flowers in Bloom

Flowers in Bloom
TEC61027

Flowers in Bloom
TEC61027

Flowers in Bloom
TEC61027

Cowboy Curt's Capitals

Pages 25–36

Materials:

scissors
glue
10" x 13" envelope
resealable plastic bag

Preparing the center:

1. Tear out the student directions, center mat, and center cards on pages 27–36.
2. Glue the student directions (page 27) on the envelope. If desired, laminate the center mat and cards on pages 29–36.
3. Cut out the cards and place them in the bag.
4. Make copies of the reproducible parent page on page 26.
5. Store the center mat, bag, and a copy of the parent page inside the envelope.

Using the center:

Have the student follow the directions on the envelope. Provide assistance as needed. After he completes the center activity, have the student take home a copy of the parent page.

25

Dear Parent,
    We have been having a rootin'-tootin' good time matching uppercase letters! Ask your child to draw a line between each letter on the left to its match on the right.

B   L
R   B
L   E
E   R

Cowboy Curt's Capitals

Here's what you do:

1. Choose a letter.

2. Find its match.

3. Put the pair on the mat.

4. Check.

5. Repeat.

A, B, C, D, E, F, G ...

Cowboy Curt's Capitals

Cowboy Curt's Capitals

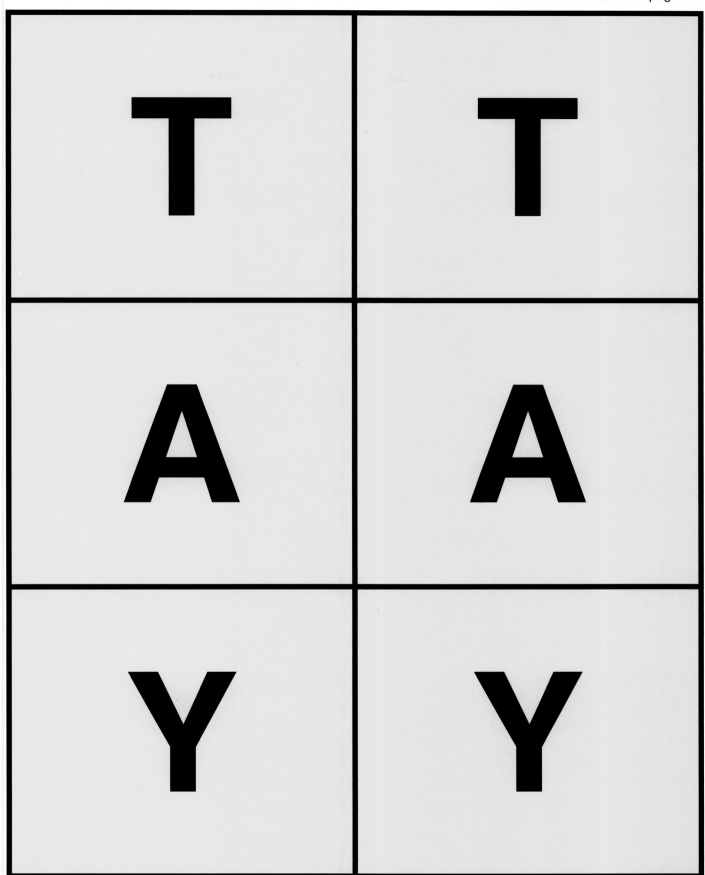

Cowboy Curt's Capitals
TEC61027

Cowboy Curt's Capitals
TEC61027

Cowboy Curt's Capitals
TEC61027

Cowboy Curt's Capitals
TEC61027

Cowboy Curt's Capitals
TEC61027

Cowboy Curt's Capitals
TEC61027

D D

Z Z

J J

Cowboy Curt's Capitals
TEC61027

Cowboy Curt's Capitals
TEC61027

Cowboy Curt's Capitals
TEC61027

Cowboy Curt's Capitals
TEC61027

Cowboy Curt's Capitals
TEC61027

Cowboy Curt's Capitals
TEC61027

M	M
S	S
P	P

Cowboy Curt's Capitals
TEC61027

Cowboy Curt's Capitals
TEC61027

Cowboy Curt's Capitals
TEC61027

Cowboy Curt's Capitals
TEC61027

Cowboy Curt's Capitals
TEC61027

Cowboy Curt's Capitals
TEC61027

Lowercase Lemonade

Pages 37–48

Materials:
scissors
glue
10" x 13" envelope
resealable plastic bag

Preparing the center:

1. Tear out the student directions, center mat, and center cards on pages 39–48.
2. Glue the student directions (page 39) on the envelope. If desired, laminate the center mat and cards on pages 41–48.
3. Cut out the cards and place them in the bag.
4. Make copies of the reproducible parent page on page 38.
5. Store the center mat, bag, and copies of the parent page inside the envelope.

Using the center:

Have the student follow the directions on the envelope. Provide assistance as needed. After she completes the center activity, have the student take home a copy of the parent page.

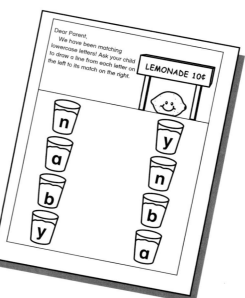

Dear Parent,
    We have been matching lowercase letters! Ask your child to draw a line from each letter on the left to its match on the right.

LEMONADE 10¢

n

a

b

y

y

n

b

a

©The Mailbox® • *Envelope Centers: Literacy* • TEC61027

38 **Note to the teacher:** Use with the directions on page 37.

Lowercase Lemonade

Here's what you do:

1. Choose a letter.

2. Find its match.

3. Put the pair on the glass.

4. Check.

5. Repeat.

Lowercase Lemonade

Lowercase Lemonade

h	h
f	f
k	k

Lowercase Lemonade
TEC61027

Lowercase Lemonade
TEC61027

Lowercase Lemonade
TEC61027

Lowercase Lemonade
TEC61027

Lowercase Lemonade
TEC61027

Lowercase Lemonade
TEC61027

44

Lowercase Lemonade

e	e
r	**r**
g	**g**

Lowercase Lemonade
TEC61027

Lowercase Lemonade
TEC61027

Lowercase Lemonade
TEC61027

Lowercase Lemonade
TEC61027

Lowercase Lemonade
TEC61027

Lowercase Lemonade
TEC61027

Lowercase Lemonade

d	d
i	i
m	m

Lowercase Lemonade
TEC61027

Lowercase Lemonade
TEC61027

Lowercase Lemonade
TEC61027

Lowercase Lemonade
TEC61027

Lowercase Lemonade
TEC61027

Lowercase Lemonade
TEC61027

Starring...Rhymes!

Pages 49–58

Materials:

scissors
glue
10" x 13" envelope
resealable plastic bag

Preparing the center:

1. Tear out the student directions, center mat, and center cards on pages 51–58.
2. Glue the student directions (page 51) on the envelope. If desired, laminate the center mat and cards on pages 53–58.
3. Cut out the cards and place them in the bag.
4. Make copies of the reproducible parent page on page 50.
5. Store the center mat, bag, and copies of the parent page inside the envelope.

Using the center:

Have the student follow the directions on the envelope. Provide assistance as needed. After he completes the center activity, have the student take home a copy of the parent page.

Starring...Rhymes!

Here's what you do:

1. Choose a card.
2. Find its match.
3. Put the pair on the mat.
4. Check.
5. Repeat.

Dear Parent,
We have been matching rhyming pictures. Ask your child to look at the picture in each star below and find the matching picture in each row. Then, if desired, have your child color each pair of pictures a different color.

Dear Parent,

We have been matching rhyming pictures. Ask your child to look at the picture in each star below and find the matching picture in each row. Then, if desired, have your child color each pair of pictures a different color.

©The Mailbox® • *Envelope Centers: Literacy* • TEC61027

50 **Note to the teacher:** Use with the directions on page 49.

Starring...Rhymes!

Here's what you do:

1. Choose a card.

2. Find its match.

3. Put the pair on the mat.

4. Check.

5. Repeat.

Starring...Rhymes!

54

Starring...Rhymes!

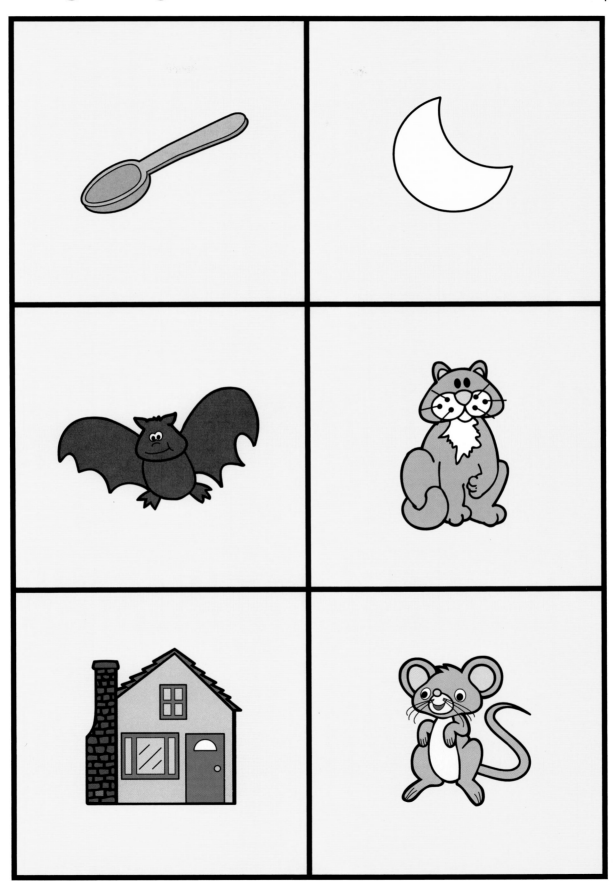

Starring...Rhymes!
TEC61027

Starring...Rhymes!
TEC61027

Starring...Rhymes!
TEC61027

Starring...Rhymes!
TEC61027

Starring...Rhymes!
TEC61027

Starring...Rhymes!
TEC61027

Starring...Rhymes!

Starring...Rhymes!
TEC61027

Starring...Rhymes!
TEC61027

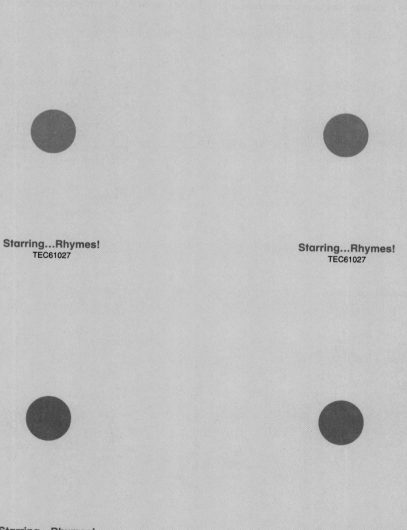

Starring...Rhymes!
TEC61027

Starring...Rhymes!
TEC61027

Starring...Rhymes!
TEC61027

Starring...Rhymes!
TEC61027

Rub-a-Dub Tub

Pages 59–68

Materials:

scissors
glue
10" x 13" envelope
resealable plastic bag

Preparing the center:

1. Tear out the student directions, center mat, and center cards on pages 61–68.
2. Glue the student directions (page 61) on the envelope. If desired, laminate the center mat and cards on pages 63–68.
3. Cut out the cards and place them in the bag.
4. Make copies of the reproducible parent page on page 60.
5. Store the center mat, bag, and copies of the parent page inside the envelope.

Using the center:

Have the student follow the directions on the envelope. Provide assistance as needed. After she completes the center activity, have the student take home a copy of the parent page.

Dear Parent,
    We have been matching rhyming pictures.
Have your child look at each row of bubbles
below. Ask him or her to color the two bubbles
in each row that show rhyming pictures.

Note to the teacher: Use with the directions on page 59.

Rub-a-Dub Tub

Here's what you do:

1. Choose a card.

2. Find its match.

3. Put the cards on the tub.

4. Check.

5. Repeat.

Rub-a-Dub Tub

Rub~a~Dub Tub

Rub-a-Dub Tub
TEC61027

Rub-a-Dub Tub
TEC61027

Rub-a-Dub Tub
TEC61027

Rub-a-Dub Tub
TEC61027

Rub-a-Dub Tub
TEC61027

Rub-a-Dub Tub
TEC61027

Rub~a~Dub Tub

Rub-a-Dub Tub
TEC61027

Rub-a-Dub Tub
TEC61027

Rub-a-Dub Tub
TEC61027

Rub-a-Dub Tub
TEC61027

Rub-a-Dub Tub
TEC61027

Rub-a-Dub Tub
TEC61027

Identifying rhyming pictures

Royal Rhyming

Pages 69–78

Materials:

scissors
glue
10" x 13" envelope
resealable plastic bag

Preparing the center:

1. Tear out the student directions, center mat, and center cards on pages 71–78.
2. Glue the student directions (page 71) on the envelope. If desired, laminate the center mat and cards on pages 73–78.
3. Cut out the cards and place them in the bag.
4. Make copies of the reproducible parent page on page 70.
5. Store the center mat, bag, and copies of the parent page inside the envelope.

Using the center:

Have the student follow the directions on the envelope. Provide assistance as needed. After he completes the center activity, have the student take home a copy of the parent page.

69

Dear Parent,
    We have been matching rhyming pictures. Have your child look at the gems in each crown. Ask him or her to color the two gems in each row that show rhyming pictures.

Note to the teacher: Use with the directions on page 69.

Royal Rhyming

Here's what you do:

1. Choose a card.

2. Find its match.

3. Put the cards in the castle.

4. Check.

5. Repeat.

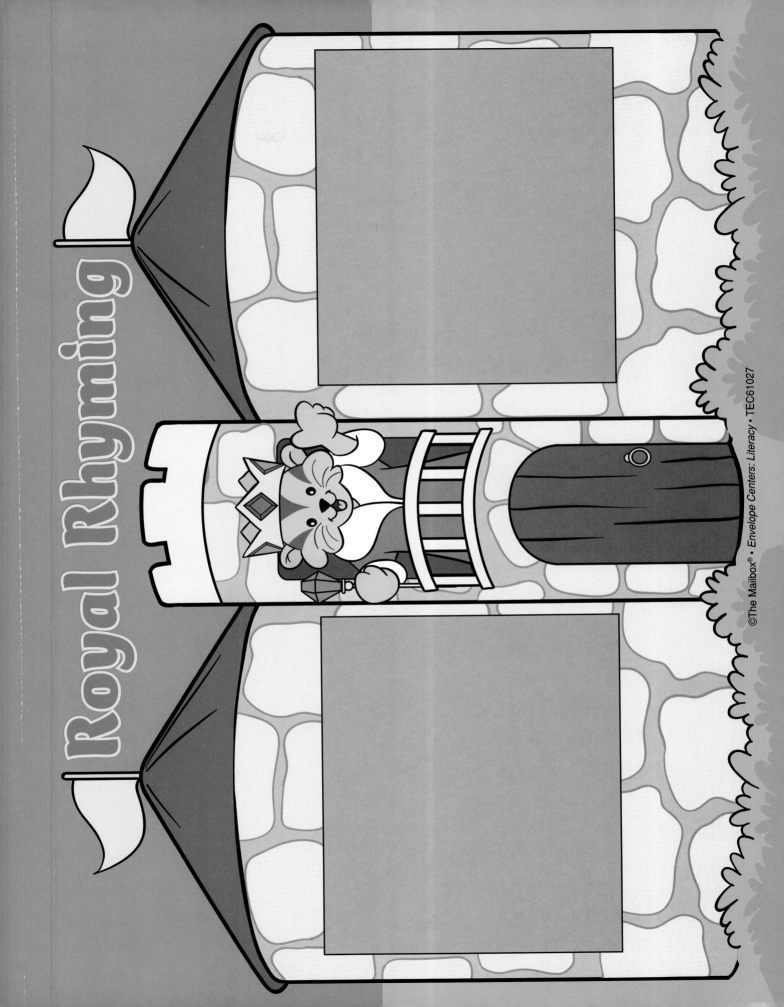

Royal Rhyming

74

Royal Rhyming

Royal Rhyming
TEC61027

Royal Rhyming
TEC61027

Royal Rhyming
TEC61027

Royal Rhyming
TEC61027

Royal Rhyming
TEC61027

Royal Rhyming
TEC61027

Royal Rhyming

Royal Rhyming
TEC61027

Royal Rhyming
TEC61027

Royal Rhyming
TEC61027

Royal Rhyming
TEC61027

Royal Rhyming
TEC61027

Royal Rhyming
TEC61027

Mouse's Masterpiece

Pages 79–88

Materials:

scissors
glue
10" x 13" envelope
resealable plastic bag

Preparing the center:

1. Tear out the student directions, center mat, and center cards on pages 81–88.
2. Glue the student directions (page 81) on the envelope. If desired, laminate the center mat and cards on pages 83–88.
3. Cut out the cards and place them in the bag.
4. Make copies of the reproducible parent page on page 80.
5. Store the center mat, bag, and copies of the parent page inside the envelope.

Using the center:

Have the student follow the directions on the envelope. Provide assistance as needed. After she completes the center activity, have the student take home a copy of the parent page.

Dear Parent,

We have been listening for the sound of the letter *m.* Help your child say the name of each picture below and decide whether it begins as *mouse* does.

Note to the teacher: Use with the directions on page 79.

Mouse's Masterpiece

Here's what you do:

1. Choose a card.

2. Name the picture.

3. If it begins like , put it on the mat.

4. Check.

5. Repeat.

82

Mouse's Masterpiece

Mouse's Masterpiece

Mouse's Masterpiece
TEC61027

Mouse's Masterpiece
TEC61027

Mouse's Masterpiece
TEC61027

Mouse's Masterpiece
TEC61027

Mouse's Masterpiece
TEC61027

Mouse's Masterpiece
TEC61027

Mouse's Masterpiece

Mouse's Masterpiece
TEC61027

Mouse's Masterpiece
TEC61027

Mouse's Masterpiece
TEC61027

Mouse's Masterpiece
TEC61027

Mouse's Masterpiece
TEC61027

Mouse's Masterpiece
TEC61027

Silly Seal

Pages 89–98

Materials:

scissors
glue
10" x 13" envelope
resealable plastic bag

Preparing the center:

1. Tear out the student directions, center mat, and center cards on pages 91–98.
2. Glue the student directions (page 91) on the envelope. If desired, laminate the center mat and cards on pages 93–98.
3. Cut out the cards and place them in the bag.
4. Make copies of the reproducible parent page on page 90.
5. Store the center mat, bag, and copies of the parent page inside the envelope.

Using the center:

Have the student follow the directions on the envelope. Provide assistance as needed. After he completes the center activity, have the student take home a copy of the parent page.

Identifying beginning sound /s/

Silly Seal

Here's what you do:

1. Choose a card.
2. Name the picture.
3. If it begins like 🦭, put it on the ball.
4. Repeat.
5. Check.

Dear Parent,
We have been listening for the sound of the letter *s*. Help your child say the name of each picture below and decide whether it begins as *seal* does.

Dear Parent,

   We have been listening for the sound of the letter *s*. Help your child say the name of each picture below and decide whether it begins as *seal* does.

Silly Seal

Here's what you do:

1. Choose a card.

2. Name the picture.

3. If it begins like , put it on the ball.

4. Repeat.

5. Check.

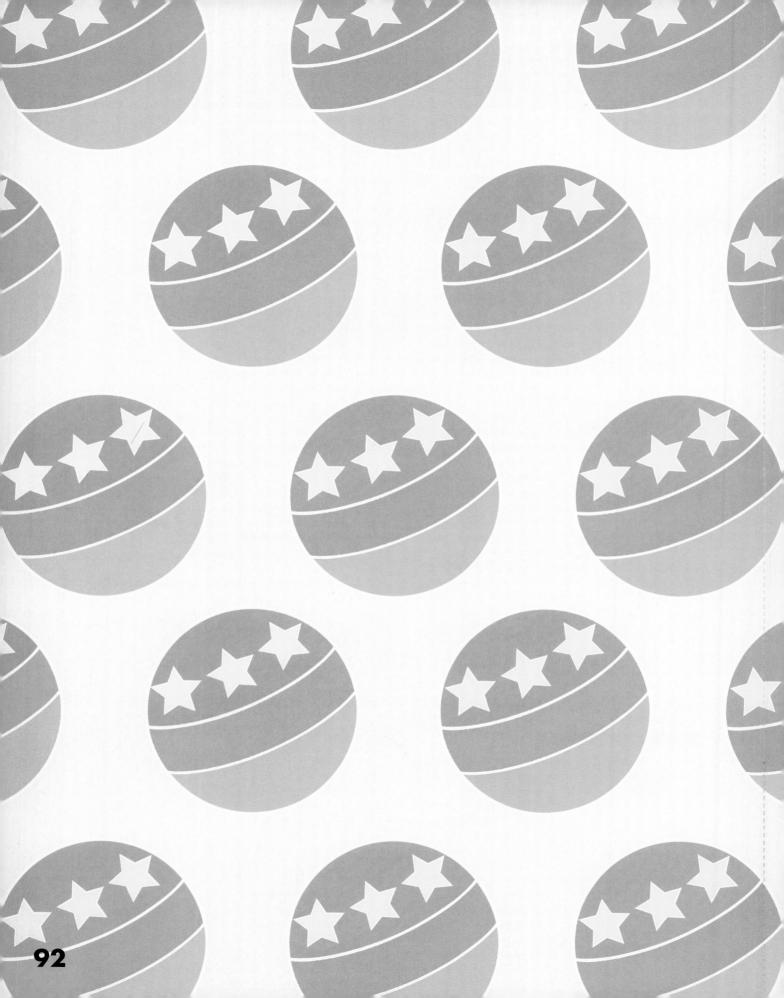

Silly
Seal

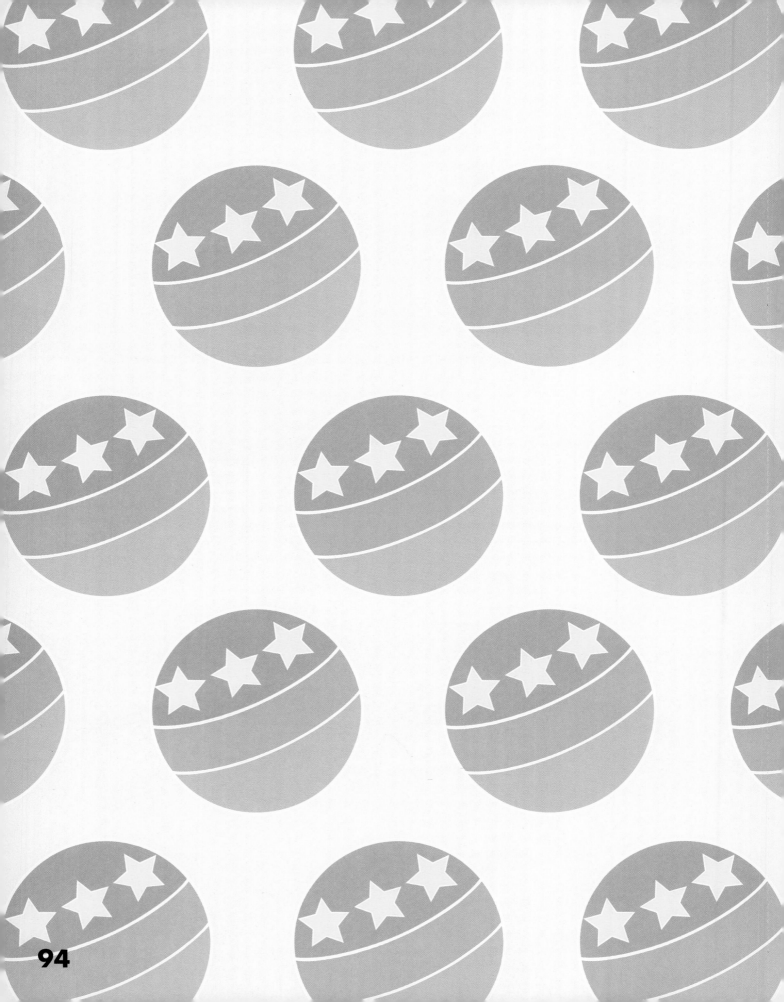

Silly Seal
TEC61027

Silly Seal
TEC61027

Silly Seal
TEC61027

Silly Seal
TEC61027

Silly Seal
TEC61027

Silly Seal
TEC61027

Silly Seal
TEC61027

Silly Seal
TEC61027

Silly Seal
TEC61027

Silly Seal
TEC61027

Silly Seal
TEC61027

Silly Seal
TEC61027

Fox's Football

Pages 99–108

Materials:

scissors
glue
10" x 13" envelope
resealable plastic bag

Preparing the center:

1. Tear out the student directions, center mat, and center cards on pages 101–108.
2. Glue the student directions (page 101) on the envelope. If desired, laminate the center mat and cards on pages 103–108.
3. Cut out the cards and place them in the bag.
4. Make copies of the reproducible parent page on page 100.
5. Store the center mat, bag, and copies of the parent page inside the envelope.

Using the center:

Have the student follow the directions on the envelope. Provide assistance as needed. After she completes the center activity, have the student take home a copy of the parent page.

Dear Parent,

We have been listening for the sound of the letter *f.* Help your child say the name of each picture below and decide whether it begins as *fox* does.

©The Mailbox® • *Envelope Centers: Literacy* • TEC61027

100 Note to the teacher: Use with the directions on page 99.

Fox's Football

Here's what you do:

1. Choose a card.

2. Name the picture.

3. If it begins like , put it on the football.

4. Repeat.

5. Check.

Fox's Football

Fox's Football

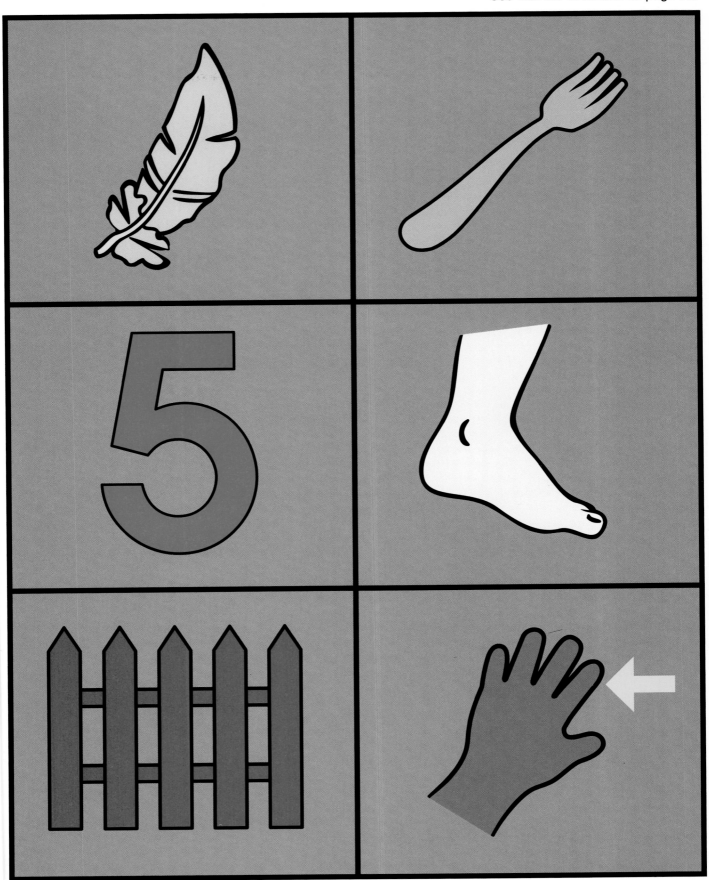

Fox's Football
TEC61027

Fox's Football
TEC61027

Fox's Football
TEC61027

Fox's Football
TEC61027

Fox's Football
TEC61027

Fox's Football
TEC61027

106

Fox's Football

Fox's Football
TEC61027

Fox's Football
TEC61027

Fox's Football
TEC61027

Fox's Football
TEC61027

Fox's Football
TEC61027

Fox's Football
TEC61027

Lion's Lollipop

Pages 109–118

Materials:

scissors
glue
10" x 13" envelope
resealable plastic bag

Preparing the center:

1. Tear out the student directions, center mat, and center cards on pages 111–118.
2. Glue the student directions (page 111) on the envelope. If desired, laminate the center mat and cards on pages 113–118.
3. Cut out the cards and place them in the bag.
4. Make copies of the reproducible parent page on page 110.
5. Store the center mat, bag, and copies of the parent page inside the envelope.

Using the center:

Have the student follow the directions on the envelope. Provide assistance as needed. After he completes the center activity, have the student take home a copy of the parent page.

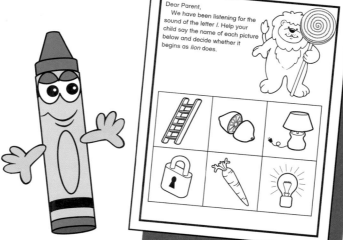

109

Dear Parent,
    We have been listening for the sound of the letter *l*. Help your child say the name of each picture below and decide whether it begins as *lion* does.

Note to the teacher: Use with the directions on page 109.

Lion's Lollipop

Here's what you do:

1. Choose a card.

2. Name the picture.

3. If it begins like , put it on the lollipop.

4. Repeat.

5. Check.

Lion's Lollipop

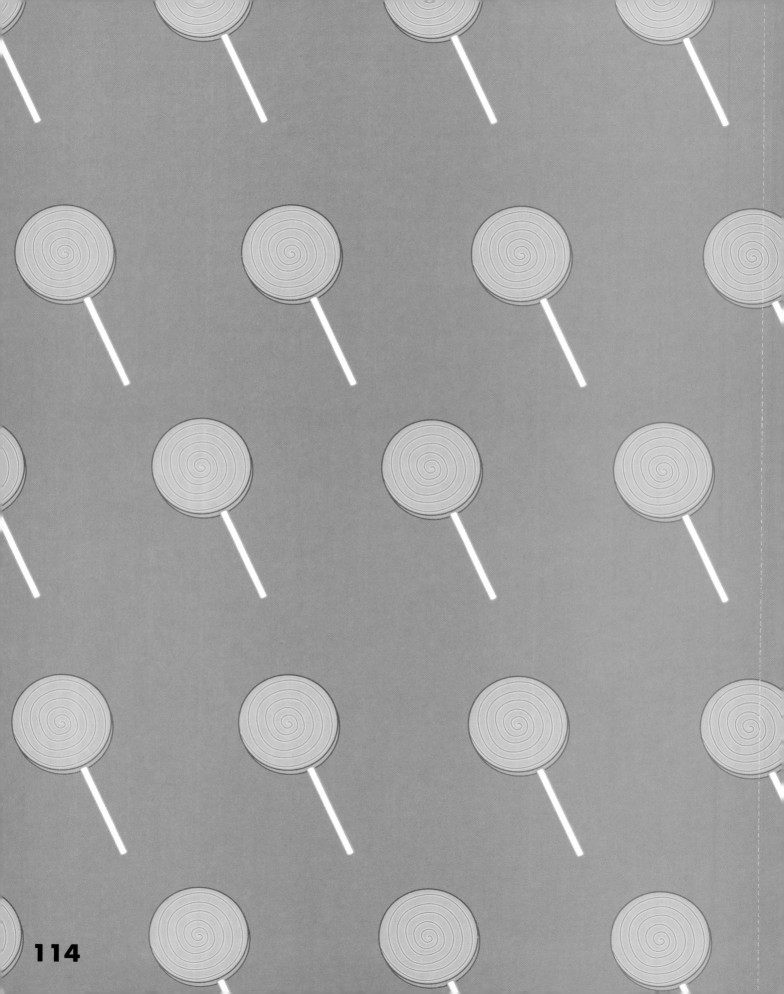

Lion's Lollipop

Lion's Lollipop
TEC61027

Lion's Lollipop
TEC61027

Lion's Lollipop
TEC61027

Lion's Lollipop
TEC61027

Lion's Lollipop
TEC61027

Lion's Lollipop
TEC61027

Lion's Lollipop

Lion's Lollipop
TEC61027

Lion's Lollipop
TEC61027

Lion's Lollipop
TEC61027

Lion's Lollipop
TEC61027

Lion's Lollipop
TEC61027

Lion's Lollipop
TEC61027

What's in the Nest?

Pages 119–128

Materials:

scissors
glue
10" x 13" envelope
resealable plastic bag

Preparing the center:

1. Tear out the student directions, center mat, and center cards on pages 121–128.
2. Glue the student directions (page 121) on the envelope. If desired, laminate the center mat and cards on pages 123–128.
3. Cut out the cards and place them in the bag.
4. Make copies of the reproducible parent page on page 120.
5. Store the center mat, bag, and copies of the parent page inside the envelope.

Using the center:

Have the student follow the directions on the envelope. Provide assistance as needed. After she completes the center activity, have the student take home a copy of the parent page.

Dear Parent,

   We have been listening for the sound of the letter *n*. Help your child say the name of each picture below and decide whether it begins as *nest* does.

©The Mailbox® • *Envelope Centers: Literacy* • TEC61027

120 **Note to the teacher:** Use with the directions on page 119.

What's in the Nest?

Here's what you do:

1. Choose a card.

2. Name the picture.

3. If it begins like , put it on the nest.

4. Repeat.

5. Check.

What's in the Nest?

What's in the Nest?

What's in the Nest?
TEC61027

What's in the Nest?
TEC61027

What's in the Nest?
TEC61027

What's in the Nest?
TEC61027

What's in the Nest?
TEC61027

What's in the Nest?
TEC61027

What's in the Nest?

What's in the Nest?
TEC61027

What's in the Nest?
TEC61027

What's in the Nest?
TEC61027

What's in the Nest?
TEC61027

What's in the Nest?
TEC61027

What's in the Nest?
TEC61027